WHAT IF WE STAYED

WHAT IF WE STAYED

SOPHEAK TOUCH
AS TOLD TO TARYN GOLDSMITH

Sopheak leaned against his car, soaking up the warm Georgia sun. Shifting his gaze back and forth along the tree-lined street, he took a moment to bask in the tranquility that the change of scenery provided. He was a long way from where he resided in the Northeast region of the United States and it felt good. Taking a long drag of his cigarette he felt an overwhelming sense of gratitude. He took great pride in the life that he had built for himself. He was a successful entrepreneur, homeowner, husband, and father. Having grown up in the city of Philadelphia, he had beaten the odds. While he was content with what he had amassed, he was just as excited about the potential for him to do more.

Inside, his family was having a good time, making memories that would last forever. Everyone was busy with their individual careers and families these days, making it hard to be a part of one another's daily lives. But gatherings like the one they had today nurtured their sense of belonging. Getting together was an unspoken reminder that their most prominent supporters were each other and that no matter where life led them they could count on one another to celebrate their wins and offer support through adversity.

Taking the final puff of his cigarette, Sopheak flicked the butt into the street and casually strolled toward his parents' front door. Just inside, he was welcomed by the nourishing sounds of family. Playful laughter and robust murmurs of conversation penetrated the air along with the aroma of authentic Cambodian cuisine. Moving through the house, he passed the living room where the children were scattered about playing.

In the kitchen, the scene was set like a snapshot from a magazine. He stared longingly as his wife stood alongside his mom and sisters preparing the food. His stomach rumbled lightly in anticipation of their meal, but the warmth that he felt in his heart was enough to stave off the hunger. He stood against the wall and admired the women at work. He caught eye contact with his mother and for a moment it was like time froze. Her face lit up when she smiled at him. The look in her eyes was reassuring, he knew she was proud of him and just as grateful for the moment. It was enough to bring tears to his eyes.

His father, Sam, sat in the recliner watching

his grandchildren in awe. They played amongst themselves without a care, knowing nothing of the gift that their lives represented. Originating from a perceived deficit, Sam had achieved the American dream. The harrowing expedition that they endured had not been in vain, for a look at their family nearly forty years later, resembled nothing of what they had been through.

The sun was setting as the family gathered for dinner. The table was laden with traditional Cambodian dishes, such as amok trei, num banh chok, and mango sticky rice. The children chattered excitedly as they waited for their food to be served, while the adults caught up on each other's lives. Sopheak was humbled to silence as he took inventory of the three generations sitting around the table. Family gatherings were normal, but something about this one was different. Unsure if he was the only one who felt a sudden overwhelming sense of pride, Sopheak declined to speak on it and just allowed himself to be in the moment.

As the meal progressed, the conversation turned to more serious topics. The elders talked about the political situation in Cambodia, while the younger

3

generation discussed their hopes and dreams for the future. But even when the conversation was serious, there was always an underlying sense of warmth and camaraderie.

*A*fter dinner, the family gathered in the living room to relax and chat. The children busied themselves with toys and electronic devices while the adults listened to music and continued their everchanging conversations. The older children listened in as the elders shared stories about their childhood in Cambodia.

By the time the night was over, everyone was feeling tired but content. They had spent time with loved ones, eaten delicious food, and laughed until their sides hurt. It was a perfect way to end the day.

Sopheak sat on the couch next to his wife and across from his brother, cradling the youngest of his three children in his arms. He watched as his eldest son sat on the floor next to his father's chair with his ipad propped up so that his grandfather could watch along. From his seat, he could see images of Cambodia shuffling across the screen as his father and son engaged in deep conversation about what they were viewing. Sopheak beamed with pride when he realized what was happening.

He watched as his son was fascinated by his grandfather's tales of life in Cambodia before the war. He asked questions about the food they ate, the clothes they wore, and the games they played.

Sam was happy to answer his grandson's questions. He told him about the rice fields they worked in, the temples they visited, and the festivals they celebrated.

Sopheak thought back to the stories that he had been told, when he learned of the sacrifices that many people like his parents made to give their children a chance at a better life. In that moment he realized just how important those sacrifices were. He watched the intergenerational exchange happening between his father and son with tears forming in his eyes thinking to himself, "What if we stayed?"

*C*ambodia had been under siege for a long time, with the control changing hands a few different times. In 1974 the Khmer Rouge had gained a substantial amount of territory thereby defeating the Cambodian government in a war that had been long established.

Under the guise of liberating the Cambodian people, the Khmer Rouge carried out a plan to implement a classless society. According to their communist beliefs, the ideal lifestyle was that of poor agricultural workers. Qualified professionals like lawyers, doctors, and teachers were perceived as a threat to the regime. Robbed of their basic human rights, the Cambodian people were forced into a life of servitude. There was no freedom of choice, they didn't even have a say in what they wore and ate, they could barely think for themselves. Food was rationed at the behest of the soldiers who were in power. Factories, hospitals, and schools were shut down and cities were evacuated. Enforced agricultural labor became the way of life for everyone including children. Families were separated, some never to see each other again. The least amount of resistance would result in torture and death. Many people died from execution, starvation, *disease, and exhaustion from being overworked.*

*I*t was November 1979, and the guards were changing again. The Vietnamese troops had arrived and were defeating the Khmer Rouge, gaining control of the majority of the country. The Vietnamese presence was helpful because it helped to release the Cambodian people from the terror of the Khmer Rouge. However, the ongoing fighting meant that they would continue to suffer through starvation.

The Vietnamese troops were welcomed by many Cambodians, who saw them as liberators. However, the fighting between the Vietnamese and the Khmer Rouge continued, and many Cambodians were caught in the crossfire. The country was in ruins, and there was widespread hunger.

The Vietnamese eventually defeated the Khmer Rouge, but the damage had been done. Millions of Cambodians had been killed, and the country was in a state of chaos. The Vietnamese presence helped to stabilize the country, but it also led to resentment among some Cambodians.

It would take a long time for the scars of the war to heal and the Cambodian people would *continue to suffer for many years after the fall of the Khmer Rouge, leaving many in search of refuge.*

*O*ne night laying with his family in their thatched hut, Sam thought about his conversation with some of the other men about leaving the village the following night. He knew that it was now or never, in all of these years he had never felt more strongly about it. They didn't have any resources, not even food, it was like they were being condemned to malnutrition and starvation. He had to do what was best for his family. As he lay awake that night he could think of nothing more than saving his family. All he could think about was giving his children the chance to grow up in a place that was not torn by war, that did not call for their starvation, suffering, or death. He would just have to inform his wife in the morning.

Sam woke up many times throughout the night, looking over his family as they lay asleep. He had made up his mind. He was going to do whatever it would take to get them to the refugee camp. There were so many dangers lurking in the jungle that they needed to cross to make it to the Thai border. But the refugee camps were their only chance and the jungle was their only way there. The years that they spent living under the Khmer Rouge's reign of terror had been nothing short of petrifying. The anguish of their grim reality was indescribable. With little food available to them and an even smaller amount of hope, his decision to brave the conditions of their journey was a no-brainer.

*I*n the morning, he told his wife about the plan to leave. There was no opposition from her. She was just as eager to flee the harsh circumstances of their homeland. Trying to ration what little food that they could find to feed their family was stressful and most times left her feeling defeated. She didn't know how long it would take them to reach the camp, or if they would make it all of the way there, but she was willing to follow her husband's lead. The alternative of staying put was just as risky as leaving and if there was such a thing as the lesser of two evils, the safety and sustenance that the camps were rumored to provide was their best bet.

*T*hey made their way from the village to the jungle under the cloak of the darkness of night. They were part of a group of families traveling toward the border. The dangers were plenty, but determination outweighed the dangers. Sam carried a stick over his shoulder with their supplies wrapped in a sac at the end. They didn't have much, just a little bit of rice and salt, probably just enough to give the girls a scoop or two every so often for sustenance. In the opposite arm, he carried his five-month-old son. His wife kept close to his pace leading their daughters by hand. As they approached the jungle and ventured in they were completely enveloped by darkness. They stepped carefully, following the steps of the person in front of them, mindful of booby traps and land mines that had been placed by the soldiers. They were especially careful to be as quiet as possible.

Sam held his son tight hoping that the motion from him walking would keep him asleep. He was trying to keep up with the group, step carefully and keep an eye on his wife as she walked behind him with their daughters. There were other families with small children moving through with them and he could only imagine that their focus was just as spread out as his own. In the distance, they could hear occasional gunshots, all around them were the lively sounds of the jungle at night.

As they progressed deeper into the jungle it got darker and darker, almost impossible to even see anything in front of you. With sight muted, the sound seemed to be amplified. All around them the sounds of the creatures of the jungle were distinct. Without trying they could hear the croaking, hissing, slithering, chirping and hooting. As they moved past vegetation, they could hear the rustling of the leaves, the hollow clunk of things falling from the trees and in the distance the sound of running water brought tranquility to a truly chaotic situation.

*T*hey had been walking for a long while, and blue light was starting to crack through the sky and cast down through the leaves of the trees. Unsure of how far they had come, everyone was noticeably fatigued. The entire group came to a sudden stop. The man in front of Sam turned to him and in a low whisper let him know that they were going to need to hide. Up in the front of the line, they had heard the sounds of soldiers marching nearby. They had to find a place to hide for a little bit. Sam motioned to Srey and they found a nearby tree to rest against. The timing was perfect, their son was wide awake and starting to get antsy.

As Srey settled against the tree, Sam handed their son to her. He was starting to squirm and smack his lips, obviously hungry. Before he could let out a cry that could expose the entire group to danger, she pulled her shirt up and put him to breast for feeding. His body relaxed immediately and he calmed down while he nursed. Srey was exhausted. She was surprised that her son was able to get anything from her because she was extremely thirsty. She was looking around her to see if there was a puddle or any type of water source in their immediate area. Her daughters

17

sat beside her against the tree while Sam opened up his sack and divided up the little cooked rice they had between the two of them. There was not enough food for them to share with their children, but they were okay with that. It was most important for the kids to get a little something to put on their stomach.

While they ate, Sam started digging a ditch for his family to hide. He didn't know how long they would have to hide and he did not want to take a chance at being found by soldiers or anyone else. His body was tired, but the adrenaline pumping through his veins helped him to push through with his digging. Once the kids were fed, Sam helped the girls into the ditch to lay down and placed his son beside his sisters. The children needed to get some rest while they could, there was still a long journey ahead. He turned back to his wife still resting against the tree trunk, obviously exhausted. She motioned toward her throat indicating her thirst. Sam immediately threw a light coating of dirt over his kids in the ditch to conceal their whereabouts. Then he got up and walked carefully looking to see where he could try to get some water for his wife. A few feet away from the tree where they were resting, there was a puddle of muddy water. Looking back toward his wife, he discreetly waved her over to him. He stood by her, keeping an eye on the area where the kids were laying as she tried to quench her thirst.

Srey kneeled next to the puddle while her husband stood to watch. It was a small muddy puddle and as she leaned in closer she realized that it smelled of dung. Dire thirst and her desire to survive made her overlook the condition of the water, she just wanted to get hydrated. She cupped her hand and gently placed it below the surface of the water, leaning forward to drink from her hand. She didn't think about the taste, she was just thankful to have something to drink. She drank a little more before standing to get back to the tree with her children. Sam insisted that she rest with the children while he kept watch. Srey was able to slide in the ditch next to her children. Sam scooped more coating of dirt over top of his family and then settled himself back against the tree.

*O*ther families were huddled around nearby trees and bushes in the thick patch of jungle where they had settled. Many of the women and children were trying to sleep or rest as much as they could, many of the men were on guard. They all stayed low but were hypervigilant about their surroundings. The anxiety in the air could be cut with a knife. They had so much to look out for and as exhausted as they were they would all rather keep moving than to be still like sitting ducks.

They sat quiet for a long time before they heard what sounded like an army of footsteps coming their way. Fear suddenly permeated everyone in the group. It was obvious in everyone's expression. Sam slid down to be closer to the ground. He wondered who was approaching their area and if they already knew that they were there. It could have been anybody, the Vietnamese soldiers, the Khmer Rouge soldiers, Thai robbers. Each of those choices held a different fate, but the worst may have been the Khmer Rouge, because there was no doubt that they would shoot on sight. As the sound of the steps moved closer, Sam held his breath. He kept his eyes peeled hoping to get a peek at who it was without them seeing him.

The footsteps seemed to be right over top of them. Sam was lying so still that he couldn't even crane his neck to get a look at who it was or where they were exactly. Thankfully, the footsteps never stopped in their area, they continued on past them. Everyone stayed still until the footsteps could be heard in the distance. Then slowly, the men started to stand and gather their families. The man who had been leading them was standing and motioning for everyone to get ready. Within minutes the group had assembled.

Sam held his son with his stick and sack thrown over his shoulder. Srey held the girls by their hands. Sam turned around briefly and leaned into his family. "No matter what happens, keep going. Don't look back no matter what. You got it?" His daughters looked up at him shaking their heads. Srey's understanding showed in her eyes. She was exhausted, but determined.

*A*s they started back out on their journey they fell back in line and tried to match the steps of the person in front of them. It was daylight and the jungle was even more lively than it was at night. There was constant gunfire and intermittent shrieks and screams of people in agony. In the daylight you could also see bodies strewn along the way. Some were military and others were likely people who did not complete their trip to the refugee camp. The group would alternate between running and walking. Running was ideal, it would help them cover more ground, but there were several families with children who were unable to do so for long periods of time. They took a few more short hiding breaks, but for the most part they traveled all day long.

Srey used the breaks as an opportunity to breastfeed her son. The girls kept quiet, but you could tell that they were hungry and tired from the looks in their eyes. All of the children in the group had the same look in their eyes, but none of them spoke. They followed along with their parents and the group, patiently waiting for the next time they would get to eat or rest.

Night had fallen and they were still walking. Their

group had gotten smaller after a few stops. There were some people who had sick family members that needed longer rests or that knew that they would not complete the trip altogether. Some people had to leave family members and friends behind and others just got separated. Sam and his family were still in line. There was a barrage of gunfire in the distance, the head of the line kept marching toward the sound. When he was asked about another way that was less dangerous, he quickly informed them that this was the only way. They were approaching a clearing in the jungle and ran to get to the other side.

That night they found another area to hide and rest. They didn't plan to stay long, just enough time to let the kids get a little rest and then they would be on their way. They were not there long when they were approached by men with guns. They were loud and demanding valuables and money from everyone. The group was still, everyone afraid to make a sudden move. This made the men even more aggressive and they started approaching everyone.

Sam sat with his family unsure of what to do. One of the men approached and put a gun to his head demanding whatever he had. He quickly offered up money that he had tucked away in a book in his sack. The man took the money and left. Sam looked at his daughters who had watched the whole ordeal, visibly shaken. He whispered to them that everything was okay, never taking his eyes off of the men who were approaching some of the other people, taking everything that they could before they fled. When they were gone, silence remained among the group. They waited until they thought that they were out of the area before they got up and continued on their way, they didn't want to take the chance of being in the same place in case they decided to return.

By the time morning had come and they could see one another, the group was noticeably even smaller. Maybe people had gotten separated in the darkness or didn't have the strength to continue, either way, those who did remain could only worry about themselves.

Their second day in the jungle was spent mostly traveling. Still shaken from the robbery, they had agreed that it was safer if they did not take as many breaks. They had to cross rivers where there were floating bodies and blood-stained water. In spite of the blood and bodies, everyone took a moment to hydrate. They had gone much of the day and night before without any water, only sucking on leaves and roots for whatever liquid they could get from them.

There was a sudden scream from the back of the group. A woman had fallen into a booby trap, begging for help. Her husband had stopped and started pleading for someone to help him rescue her, but everyone else just kept moving forward. They could not afford to turn back. In fact, they quickened their pace, afraid that the noise would draw attention to their location.

*S*am turned his head slightly, ensuring that his wife and daughters were still on his heels, they were and he was thankful. They slowed up with the group as they entered a heavily mined area. They all whispered warnings to be careful as they tip-toed through. Night was falling and they would need to stop for a moment to rest soon. There was no way that they could continue in this area with no light to see where they were going.

They rested until there was light in the sky. This time when they went to move again there were only two families and the man who had been leading their group was gone. Sam spoke briefly with the other man who was left. Some of the others had gone out searching for food during the night and did not return. He wasn't sure of where the others were, but they decided to continue on their way. They had walked for most of the day when they were approached by a Khmer soldier with his gun drawn. Sam's heart started beating fast, they had come so far only to run into who they were running from. The soldier called Sam's name. Taking a closer look, Sam realized that he knew the soldier from his home village. His heart calmed as he begged for mercy for his family. The soldier let Sam and his family go, but told the other family to stay put.

Sam and Srey hurried away with their family. Srey's heart hurt when she thought about the fate that the other family would meet, but she was grateful that the soldier had let them go. They walked for a while before they stopped to feed the baby. While Srey fed him, Sam and the girls took a second to close their eyes and rest their bodies.

Sam cracked his eyes as the suppressed light of dusk crept through the leaves of the trees. It was time to take his family to continue on their journey. As he stood upright he turned to look around him. When they had arrived at this area earlier he was shaken and did not see the surroundings as well. He hurried to quietly gather his wife and children so that they could be on their way. They needed to keep moving. As usual, he was trying to get ahead of any dangers that could be lurking but he was also taking in how far they had come. If he was ever unsure before, he was confident that he would deliver his family to Thailand's border.

*T*he predawn light crept into the sky as Sam and his family completed their third night of travel. They had arrived at the border, now they had to make it across and into the camp. There were several other refugee families waiting along the border hoping to get across at the same time. They had to be careful not to alert the Thai soldiers who were guarding the border. Everybody sat back, waiting for the perfect opportunity to get past the soldiers and make it safely into the camp. The entrance to the camp was not far away, if they timed it right they could all make it across. The soldiers had all turned and started to retreat from their posts. Unsure of how far they were going or how long they might be gone, there was a silent consensus that this was their moment.

Sam and Srey communicated using only their eyes. They had come too far to not take the final leap. Sam secured his son while Srey quietly directed the girls to run. They needed to move quickly. There had been many stories of refugees turned away and sent back to face starvation or join the mass graves of the killing fields. Their greatest chance at survival was making it into the camp.

Placing their feet on Thai soil was like reaching the promised land. Safety was in plain sight, just a stone's throw away from the border. Moving swiftly, the group ran in a sparsely separated pack. The Thai soldiers were none the wiser as they continued their trek into the distance. Sam's family was near the front of the pack. They were nearing the camp's gate when a baby began to cry. The sound was quickly muffled but not before the soldiers turned in unison and opened fire on the group.

Running for their lives, Sam and Srey hurried to the protection of the camp. Once they had crossed the threshold of the campground, Sam came to an abrupt stop and turned to face his wife and daughters. Their journey was far from over and to be honest he had no idea what to expect would come next, but he took a moment to be thankful for making it this far. Srey let up a thankful grin, she was hungry and thirsty, but those feelings were secondary to her appreciation for having escaped the devastation in Cambodia. Walking through the campground, Sam found a place for his family to settle while he went to figure out how the camp worked. Thankful to have a moment to rest, Srey sat holding her son with her *daughters by her side. They were proud fugitives who had escaped the real threat of death in Cambodia, searching for life and the opportunity for their family to flourish. Whatever came next was worth the risk.*

*S*am moved about the front of the camp speaking with different people, in an attempt to understand what he needed to do for his family from this point. There were several tables set up to distribute food for each family. Stepping into the line that had formed, he turned around surveying the camp. There was a sea of makeshift tents and families milling about, some seemed lost while others seemed to have adjusted well to their temporary community. The first table set up had tarps and rope for sale. Sam was thankful that he still had a little bit of money stashed away. He had given serious thought to placing some money in a few different places just in case they were robbed or lost some of their things. He stepped forward to purchase the supplies to create shelter for his family, tucked it under his arm, and stepped back into the line.

An older man approached the line from the side, he asked Sam and the others who were close by if they were new. No one responded, they had all escaped the dangers of the Khmer Rouge and the jungle but they were unsure what other dangers they might face in the camp. The older man laughed and assured them that he was not there to harm anyone. Having already collected his ration of food for the day, he noticed their faces as he headed back to his tent. He told them of a well close by where they could fetch fresh water for their families. Instantly relieved, several of the men in line spoke up to thank the older man. The man introduced himself as Nhean. He had been at the camp for close to a year and was expecting to be picked up and sent to another camp any day. He gave them a brief overview of camp life and explained that the food rations that they received might go up and down based on availability. There were thousands of refugees arriving at the camp every day. He was very clear in his warning that during the day they were safe in the camp, but at night they could be visited by Thai robbers and even Khmer Rouge soldiers. The only organized services that there were food distribution and transfers, other than that, they had to fend for themselves. As he prepared to carry his ration back to his tent he gave a final warning for the newcomers to be frugal with their rations. Because they were so close to the border they were still in danger of the shooting and bombings that were happening nearby. When danger was present the relief workers would evacuate and sometimes not return for days at a time. They *needed to be prepared for those instances. Sam took in everything that Nhean mentioned and was intentional in storing that information for the survival of his family.*

*N*early a week had passed since Sam and his family arrived at the camp. They were slowly adjusting to their new life. Srey spent much of her time caring for the children near their tarp-topped tent, while Sam moved about, fetching water and other necessities for his family. They sat and slept in the dirt with the tarp protecting them from the hot sun and other weather elements. Whenever the opportunity presented itself, Sam spoke to relief workers about the options for asylum. He received very little information yet he remained vigilant. Unsure of what to expect, he put his heart into making sure his family was as comfortable as they could be. The camp was far from paradise, but they went to sleep full every night. They were content for the time being.

*T*he sea of makeshift tents grew larger and larger as thousands of refugees arrived daily. The uncertainty and crowded conditions of the camp were much more welcoming than the deplorable conditions that they had escaped in Cambodia. Families whose tents were set up nearby would commune with one another, creating small villages within the camp. It was the closest resemblance to social life and community, especially since so many people were separated from their families and friends. Those communities offered a sense of normalcy during a time of mass displacement.

*C*hantrea was Sam and Srey's neighbor to the left. She lived in her tent with her two children and her mother-in-law. Her husband didn't make it to Thailand. He was murdered in front of them by Khmer Rouge soldiers on their first night in the jungle. The soldiers had taken every one of their possessions before they dragged him a few feet away from his family, beat him, and shot him. They laughed at the look of fear that was plastered on the faces of his family before they walked away.

Chantrea's mother-in-law was ill. In fact, they didn't think that she could make the trip to Thailand. She made it, but witnessing her son's murder was more than she could handle. Since they had arrived at the camp her health was declining. Chantrea had a four-year-old son and a two-year-old daughter. Caring for two small children and her mother-in-law was difficult. With all of their possessions being taken, she was not able to afford tent supplies to protect them from extreme weather conditions. Her ill mother-in-law stayed put most of the time and in her weakened state was unable to assist her with the children. Becoming acquainted with Sam and Srey had been

43

a huge help. Srey would keep an eye on Chantrea's family when she went to stand in line for food or fetch water. She was struggling to hold everything together, but sheer determination carried her forward.

*T*o *Sam and Srey's right was a tent with three brothers. The eldest, Vanndeth, was probably nineteen or twenty, and the other two were younger teens. They pretty much stayed to themselves, looking out for one another. It was rare to find them congregating with other refugees. Sam had the opportunity to speak briefly with Vanndeth while they were on a trek for water. Vanndeth explained that their father was removed from their home years before by the Khmer Rouge and that they had never seen him again. They had never learned of his fate but assumed the worst. Their mother stayed behind but encouraged him to take his brothers to seek a better life. She had never been the same after they took her husband away and rathered to stay and face her fate in her home country. It broke his heart to leave her behind, but he feared what would happen to him and his siblings if he didn't at least try. They had arrived at the camp about two weeks before Sam and his family, but had adjusted pretty quickly.*

46

The adjustment was inevitable, camp life was the same day in and day out. They were playing a waiting game with no end in sight. Sam did not let a day go by without checking for information, but there was never anything new. He was growing anxious. Srey had informed him that she was pregnant with their fourth child, and he could only hope for better living conditions.

Over the next seven months, they weathered the storm as best they could. Every few weeks, buses would line up at the entrance of the camp, Sam always hovered nearby listening for his family's name. When the buses were full and the names stopped being called out without his family's name being included, Sam would head back to his tent reassuring himself along the way that their day would come soon. Srey was getting big and as grateful as he was for the asylum, Sam was wary about his new baby being born in the camp. Otherwise, the girls had become accustomed to their living situation. Sam knew that the transition was not easy, but he had total faith that it would be worth it. Vanndeth and his brothers were called onto a bus one day. Sam stood and watched, happy to see the brothers leaving. Vanndeth turned and waved as he stood in line to board. In the months that had passed he and Sam had become more acquainted, though his conversation was still limited.

*O*ne morning, Sam and Srey were awakened by agonizing crying and screaming. They woke to find Chantrea kneeling beside her mother-in-law who appeared to be asleep. Her children were standing next to her, barely awake just looking at their grandmother lying there. Sam stood quickly, brushing the dirt from his pants and walking toward Chantrea. As he approached standing over her, he noticed that her mother-in-law was unusually still. Stepping a little closer he realized that she was not breathing. She was dead. He gently touched Chantrea's back to offer her comfort. Chantrea had long suspected that her mother-in-law was going to die, her health had never improved since they had arrived at the camp, but she was hoping that she could hang on. All of the losses that she had experienced over the last few years were especially tragic, but losing her husband and mother-in-law while they were fleeing was more jarring than ever. Hopeless and afraid all she could do was cry. Srey got up and called for Chantrea's children to come to their tent. She laid them down next to her children and joined her husband in comforting their mother.

WHAT IF WE STAYED

52

*T*he buses lined up near the entrance to the camp, and at the same time the relief workers started to crowd around. It was the same process every time the buses would show up. Refugees headed toward the entrance in hoards, eager to hear their name called for departure or to see if any information would be given out. If they were lucky they could chat with a relief worker directly, although more often than not their questions would go unanswered. The relief workers stood facing the crowd holding their clipboards and megaphones, with their two-way radios hanging from their hips. They wore sun visors to protect them from Thailand's hot July sun. Ponchos were visibly hanging from some of the workers' back pockets in preparation for the rain that was to be expected during the season. Sam stood close to the entrance listening to the names and announcements being called out over the megaphones. Tired, he had half a mind to walk away and head back to his tent to sit down. Over the past eight months, he had stood in the same position far too many times to count, only to have to experience the gut-wrenching feeling that came about when he did not hear his name. Today would be no different, he was sure of it.

A long time had passed and names were still being called. Sam was still standing in the same place. He looked up at the sky and noticed the clouds moving in. It was the rainy season so there was no doubt in his mind that there was a storm brewing. He hoped that they were almost done for the day so that he could get back to his family and to the little shelter from the rain that his tent provided. Today he was just not up to waiting around. He did not know exactly what getting on the bus meant, there was never much information given about that. For the moment he was content and just desired to be with his family. Slowly, he started to walk away from the crowd. He had only taken a few steps when he stopped dead in his tracks. He could not believe his ears, they had called for his family. Overwhelmed, Sam could feel the tears welling up in his eyes. He took off running back to his tent to retrieve his family. His entire mood had taken a turn for the better. He still did not know much of what to expect but he knew that they were one step closer to a better life.

*S*am and Srey stood in the line to board the bus
with their children. Being in the bus line had its
perks. The relief workers actually had information to
give though it was still sparse. They informed them
that they were headed to Khao I Dang, it was another
camp, but much more civilized. They waited patiently
to reach the front of the line, where they gave their
names to another relief worker and were directed to
the appropriate bus. Srey and the girls made their way
up the stairs first while Sam carried his son up behind
them. They were both grateful to have made it this
far. Their children had grown over the months that
they had been at this camp. Things were imperfect,
to say the least, but they were able to eat daily. Now
they were looking forward to what was to come.

Stepping off of the bus at Khao I Dang, Sam immediately noticed the difference from the previous camp. He stood holding his son surveying the bamboo village with dirt roads, barbed wire, and armed guards. Things here seemed much more organized, offering a small amount of relief from the constant state of not knowing. Srey stood right beside him surveying their new surroundings and urging the girls to be still as they awaited further instruction.

When the bus was empty, the entire busload was ushered over to a group of workers standing by the fence. They were instructed to form a line to start the registration process where they would be given directions to the section where they could find their huts. That process was seamless, they moved pretty quickly through the line and were given further instructions to complete their registration and get acclimated to the camp.

That night, after they had eaten and laid the kids down for bed, Sam and Srey sat up talking about what was next. One of the things that they would eventually need to let the relief workers know was where they wanted to go. America had always been their choice and nothing had changed in that regard. They had family that had already been expatriated to America and from what they understood that would make being granted asylum even easier. Sam had to go to sit with a worker and continue their registration process in the morning, he wanted to make certain that he and his wife were on the same page.

*I*n the morning when Sam went to the front of the camp he waited patiently for a relief worker to come, to his aid. They spoke at length about his family and their wishes for expatriation. The worker assured him that there were no guarantees and no set amount of time to get things sorted out, the results generally varied per family. He did guarantee Sam that they would be at Khao-I-Dang much longer than they were at the last camp. Several different organizations would come on-site to offer resources to the refugees, including those like UNICEF and Red Cross. He gave Sam a lot of information at once. He told him where and how to get the clothes that were donated from The Red Cross, the location of the medical building, where to go to find work or skills training for himself, and how to get his children registered for school. Walking back to his hut after he met with the relief worker, Sam was content. They had an opportunity to return to a somewhat normal life.

*O*ver the next few weeks, Sam worked to get his family accustomed to their new life. Srey was very far along and would be preparing to give birth to their newest child. Since they knew that they would be here for a while, they wanted to get as close to being settled as possible. They went to the Red Cross to get some of the clothes that were donated. For so long they had worn these black uniforms, they were ecstatic to be able to discard those and wear the more colorful and vibrant clothing that was provided. Something as simple as clothing did wonders for their pride and self-esteem. Sam and Srey locked eyes after watching the girls happily twirl in their new dresses. Sam had found work as a teacher and the girls were registered for school. They decided that Srey would stay home until after she had given birth. They established their daily routine and began to explore life as refugees at Khao I Dang.

Social life at Khao I Dang was robust. With most adults working at different places throughout the camp and children attending school and playing together, you were bound to get to know a few people and start recognizing familiar faces. Religious activities were able to resume, some huts were turned into places for Buddhist ceremonies, there was a theater and even a Christian church. As they adjusted, the camp felt more and more like a home with limited freedoms. Everything that they were given came from outside help, even water and rice. They were totally dependent on the workers. Before they had to leave their homes, they had the freedom to move around as they needed to get what they needed to survive. If they needed any extra help there were family and friends who could chip in. At the camp, they were dependent on outside aid, and that coupled with the inevitable feeling of displacement was unnerving. The situation was not completely unbearable, but it did add to the already heightened stress that many people were feeling.

There were tens of thousands of people living at Khao I Dang. Sam was taken aback when he ran into his cousin Khean. It was the brightest moment that he'd had in a long time. It had been a little over a month since they had arrived at the camp, and after living in utter uncertainty for so long, he felt a great deal of gratitude. They weren't at their final destination but it would do for the time being. He was excited to reunite with someone from his family and thankful to know that they too had made it out of Cambodia. He could not wait to bring him to see Srey and the kids. When he arrived at their hut with his cousin in tow, Srey's eyes lit up. She stood up from her sitting position and immediately embraced Khean, seeing his face and knowing that he was nearby was settling. They chatted briefly about Khean's family and his work in the camp hospital.

Srey gave birth to a baby boy at the camp hospital about six weeks after they had arrived at Khao I Dang. The girls were really excited about their baby brother Sopheak. While they visited their mother and brother at the hospital, some of the workers gave the girls plastic gloves to play with. Srey was happy. She took a moment to reflect on the birth of her new son and while their situation was not exactly ideal, the promise of eventually raising her children in America kept her hopeful. Though she had never visited America, from what she'd been told it seemed like it would be paradise. All she had ever heard was about the amount of opportunity and freedom there. Some of the relief workers were from America, and there were hoards of clothing and other resources from there as well, so she could only think good thoughts.

*O*ne evening, Khean and his family came by to visit Sam, Srey, and the children. They had come to see the baby and to spend time with their family. It was the first time that they would get to sit and really talk about how they'd arrived at the camp and how their lives were progressing. Khean had arrived at Khao I Dang a few months before Sam and Srey and he too had chosen to seek asylum in America. They had made it to Thailand without being robbed or caught by any of the military factions. But Khean's eldest son who was ten had been severely injured when someone in front of him stepped on a landmine and shrapnel ended up in his lower left leg. Khean had to carry him on his back the rest of the way. By the time they were able to get medical attention, the shrapnel was too hard to find and remove. Khean's son was left with a severe limp and constant discomfort and pain. They were doing their best to help him manage, but sometimes it was difficult since he was still a young boy who wanted to run and play.

After Khean and his family left, Srey settled down to feed the baby while Sam readied the other three children for bed. Srey was tired after she'd fed the *baby, so she laid down too. Sam sat by the entryway to their hut. He wasn't tired so he decided to enjoy the night air. The only sounds he heard outside of the hut were the sounds of nature. He sat with his eyes closed and enjoyed the near silence. A feeling of calm came over him as he acknowledged that they were on their way. While they had not completed their mission, they were in the home stretch. He didn't care about the amount of time that they would spend at Khao I Dang, he was focused on the processes that were in place to help him get what he wanted. The cherry on top was the feeling of having a home for his family, however temporary, and the blessing of having family nearby.*

Sam's silence was interrupted when he heard people yelling in the distance. "Rebels! Go! Go!"

He jumped up and looked out of his hut. There were a bunch of people scrambling while others were quickly making their way out of the huts. Alarmed he woke Srey and the girls and snatched up the boys, urging them to leave the hut. Outside they joined the growing hoard of people that was growing as they moved. With no clue as to just what was happening, he was confused and slightly shaken. He called out for Srey to keep up as he cradled his sons. One of their neighbors, Sok, ran alongside him. He urged Sam to find a place to hide before he took off and sprinted ahead. Sam continued to follow the crowd that was thickening as they moved forward. He found it hard to ignore the knot that had formed in the pit of his stomach. He knew that they weren't out of the thick of the chaos, but he was definitely not expecting this. He realized that he'd been consumed by their progression and vowed to never make that mistake again. When they heard gunfire in the distance, Sok assured him that they would be fine, the Thai soldiers had arrived to chase the robbers away.

*F*or the next two years, Sam would bear the weight that each day brought. Some days were good, others were rough, as long as his entire family's lives were renewed each morning he had reason to keep moving forward. His hope remained intact.

His family was untroubled, aside from the occasional visit from robbers and rebels. The danger always occurred at night when the relief workers were away. A lot of times, the danger seemed more severe for the women. There were a lot of stories of women being abused, raped, or kidnapped. One night the rebels came in and threw a grenade into the hut of a family who had not gotten out in time. The explosion set the hut on fire killing the entire family. When night fell, being in the camp heightened their vulnerability, but it was also the only way that they could get help through the process of seeking asylum.

Sam moved on from his position as a teacher and started helping build new constructions for the camp. Srey continued doing odd jobs and caring for the boys who were both active toddlers. The girls were just growing and going with the flow. The camp at times would hold activities for the children, like art classes and other small events to give them some form of entertainment. Despite lurking dangers and limited freedoms. They enjoyed the camp but knew that they couldn't stay there forever. Everything was a matter of passing the time until they received more information about their next steps.

Khean and his family had gotten all of their paperwork done and were transported to another camp to prepare to go to America. Before they left, Khean made sure to see Sam and wish him well. They parted ways with the expectation of seeing one another in America. Sam had gone to sit with the relief workers on several different occasions. They had spent time talking about where they wanted to settle. His answer for America never wavered. Another time they met and assisted Sam through the process of writing letters for sponsorship and ensuring that they had all of the proper information for his entire family. He was waiting for his name to come up for departure. He knew that there would be a test and interview prior to leaving. But he was prepared.

During his last few meetings with relief workers, he had a translator named Rithy. Rithy had escaped

Cambodia when the Khmer Rouge first reared its ugly head, before the fall of Phnom Penh. He sought asylum in France. Although he escaped, the Khmer Rouge's reign had a heavy impact on him. Most of his family had stayed in Cambodia and for four years he worried about their existence and safety. When the border opened up in 1979, he took the time to learn to speak Thai and enlisted as a relief worker at Khao-I-Dang to serve as a translator. Rithy and Sam bonded during their meetings, for Sam, it was gratifying to speak with a worker who not only sympathized but truly understood the struggles that the campers were dealing with.

*W*hen his name came up, Sam could barely contain his excitement. He knew better than to expect much, he was not quite at the finished line yet. He showed up for his test and interview confident that he would do well. There was no other option. As he waited for his name to be called he sat thinking of all they had gone through over the last few years. It had been and was still an ordeal, but he never once felt sorry for himself, nor did he allow his family to feel that way. Things were the way they were. They had gone through this entire ordeal wanting more but never feeling sorry for themselves. They accepted and adapted to the conditions as they were. Having to leave their home was difficult but every day he saw more and more how necessary it was. Whenever he saw refugees arriving in droves at the first camp or this camp, he saw that things had not changed at home. He saw the pain and despair. He paid attention to those people who were having a difficult time mentally grasping being essentially forced from their home, losing family, or having to leave them behind in a matter of life or death. He knew that the only way out was through it and he was making his way for his family.

After taking the test and sitting for the interview, Sam and Srey were anxious to hear the outcome. Nearly a week passed before they heard anything. When they were told they would be sent to the Philippines to prepare to be sent to America, they were beside themselves with joy. They had seen so many different outcomes that even though they hoped for the best, they were also prepared to hear otherwise. Relaying the news to the girls, they spent the next few days preparing the little possessions they had for their departure.

*S*am arrived with his family at the Phillippines Refugee Processing Center during the Summer of 1983. They were flown from Thailand to Manila and then arrived at the Processing Center by bus. As they arrived at the gates they were taken through a registration process where they were told that the average stay at this camp was for six months. Some people left sooner, some later, but on average they could expect to be there for six months. They would complete tuberculosis testing and any other requirements from the powers that be. Here the refugees that were headed to the United States were offered English as a Second Language, culture training, and job orientation. Sam and Srey were humble but proud, they were headed to America, the land of opportunity. Most of the refugees here were more upbeat because unlike in the other camps where they didn't know what was to come, most people knew where they were being resettled and that it was only a matter of time.

*T*he Phillippine Refugee Processing Center housed as many as 18,000 refugees at a time. The population was comprised of refugees from Cambodia, Laos, and Vietnam. It was divided up into ten neighborhoods that each held thirty buildings that were divided up into bunkhouses, each quarter housing up to six people. Outside of individuals' quarters, there were hammocks hung and lines with clothes drying and providing shade from the hot sun. There were also clinics, hospitals, markets, a gasoline station, churches, religious temples, an Administration building, a post office, and recreation spaces. There were a few different school buildings around the camp where it was not uncommon to hear students practicing American phrases as a group if you were nearby. The refugees were also offered skills training and were taught how to engage in services for the community. Most people were trained toward being service-oriented, these skills would help once they resettled and had to learn their new communities. The camp was an Indochinese melting pot where there was an opportunity to learn at every turn. During the day you could hear a mixture of languages being spoken as people from different backgrounds moved about within the camp. At sunset, you could hear prayers being made in the temples, and at night the calming sounds of the forest seemed to surround the camp.

The Processing Center was more liberal than Khao I Dang. They were free to move about outside of the camp. With all of the training provided, there were very few opportunities for leisure at nearby beaches or in the town, but that was of no concern to Sam since his only focus was getting his family to America. They did enjoy downtime, but Sam did not prefer to be bogged down with planning and navigating outings, he preferred to spend that time learning about where they were headed. The children played amongst themselves and with other children that lived in their neighborhood. Sam got a kick out of practicing English with his children. He sometimes worried about the decisions he'd made up until that moment. He wondered if he was doing his due diligence as a parent. Although his children seemed to be content adjusting to change several times over, he hoped that either way it turned out, they knew he had made the decisions that he did to improve their lives. They had gone through so many involuntary changes in the last *few years, he wanted to be as prepared as he could for the change that he was actually seeking. He did not know what to expect of America. But his family's agility made him confident in their ability to find their way.*

They adapted to life at the Processing Center and waited their time out. It seemed like every week or two there were people leaving the camp to be resettled and others arriving to start their clock to resettlement. The constant wave of people moving in and out was motivating. There were some people whom he had run into who had been at the camp much longer than six months with no planned resettlement date in sight. There weren't many, but those circumstances were a grim possibility. He held several conversations with the refugees at the Processing Center to get a realistic idea of what his time frame would look like and get some insight on the final testing. Sam remained hopeful as he and his family moved through their coursework readying them for America.

When they successfully completed their coursework, they had to wait until they saw their names posted to find out when they would leave for America. In the meantime, they had to complete more health screenings to ensure they did not have any disease or illness before being sent to America. Once it was determined that the entire family was not ill, they waited, checking daily for the day that their names were posted with a date to leave. It seemed like weeks had passed before they finally saw Sam's name posted. It had been a long road, but they finally had a definitive answer, they were headed to have a chance at a better life.

Sam was overcome with emotion. This was all that he wanted for his family. When he had set out years before with the intention of getting his family to America, he didn't know how it would work out, he just knew that it had to work. His joy was mixed with new anxieties as he contemplated the reality of them relocating to another country. He would not fully believe that they were actually leaving until they were on the plane and moving away from the gate, and even then until he exited the plane and stepped foot on US soil. His thoughts were all over the place. What if some information comes up that makes them ineligible for resettlement? What if they don't board the right plane?

*T*he day they left the Processing Center they were taken to an airport by bus. The ride to the airport in Manila was a long one, it seemed like they would never arrive. Neither Sam nor Srey had ever been on an airplane. The prospect was both scary and exciting. They were not the only ones, other refugees on their bus to Manila had no qualms about sharing their fears and anxieties. As they were led through the airport they were in awe. Careful to keep a tight hold on the kids, they watched as thousands of people moved about some running for their flights, others taking their time scouring the shops that were set up along the way. They were a long way from Battambang in the countryside of Cambodia, and once they took their assigned seats on the plane the distance would increase tenfold.

Boarding the plane was an event in itself. The kids would ooh and aah as they walked through the tunnel onto the aircraft, led by their sponsor. Sam and the boys sat a row behind Srey, the girls, and the sponsor. They had a long flight ahead of them. Night had fallen in Manila, and as the plane ascended into the sky, Sam and his family looked out at the lighted outline of the city that was getting smaller by the second.

The flight attendants moved throughout the cabin, wearing crisp uniforms and big smiles, checking on passengers and passing out refreshments. Sam and Srey couldn't understand what they were saying, and fearful of falling ill eating while in motion, they politely declined any food. The kids eventually drifted off to sleep but Sam and Srey were wide awake thinking of what was waiting for them in America. They had spent the past few years wanting to go, and the past few months learning about the culture and getting an idea about how things worked. It was surreal that they were headed to get hands-on experience. But at the same time, they were back in a state of not knowing what was next. They would have to build a new life in America and that idea made both of them nervous. At some point, both Sam and Srey closed their eyes and tried to relax as best they could.

*T*hirteen *hours after boarding their plane in Manila,
Sam and his family arrived in Philadelphia,
Pennsylvania. It was bittersweet, with his feet planted
on American soil he took a look at his family. They
were all standing with him, everyone in relatively
good health. He looked at his daughters Dara and
Chanthy, they were four and six when they left, and
for both of their entire lives, all they had known was
a home terrorized by radicals where the only thing
certain was death. He looked at his sons, the oldest,
Sok was just a baby when they had left and his
wife was just pregnant with Sopheak. Their entire
existence had been moving from place to place, not
knowing what dangers or changes were coming their
way. He looked at his wife, he couldn't hold back his
smile. Throughout the entire journey, she'd been the
best teammate anyone could ask for. She stood by him
and she stood strong. No matter how bad things got,
no matter how scared, frustrated, and defeated she
may have felt, she pushed through determined to get
their family away from the ever-accumulating human
misery that had besieged Cambodia. They made it to
the land of freedom and opportunity, and that alone
warmed his heart but broke his soul. They were right*

back in a situation very similar to the ones that they had been navigating for the past few years. He had no clue what was next, but he was confident that they would make the best of it and adapt accordingly.

*F*ollowing their sponsor through the airport in Philadelphia, Sam glanced at every sign that he passed. He recognized some of the symbols and letters from classes that he had taken at Khao I Dang and the Processing Center in the Phillippines. As they walked, Sam caught bits and pieces of conversations. He couldn't understand anything. He looked at his wife and noticed the worried expression on her face. "We are good." He called out to her. They had escaped the worst, having no food, no rest, constant torment, and fear. They had survived living as refugees, displaced by the enlarged limbs of war. They had adjusted time and again and America would be no different.

Making their way out of the airport to a van that was waiting for them, Sam noticed how cold it was here as compared to the warm weather in Cambodia. Their sponsor told them that they would go to his house to have a meal and rest up. Riding along the highway, Sam, Srey, and all four of the kids were staring out of the windows. In the distance, you could see tall buildings that looked like they went up into the sky. As they got closer they had a perfect view of the skyline, everyone was silently awestruck by the unfamiliar beauty that surrounded them. It was really a whole new world.

Over the next couple of weeks, their sponsor took them to the necessary government buildings and businesses that they needed to visit to officially begin life here. He helped them apply for welfare so that they could get food to feed their family and have a way to get healthcare. He took them to register their children for school and showed them where they could look for work.

The Cambodians who came to South Philadelphia in the 1980s were fleeing a country that had been ravaged by war and genocide. They had lost everything, and they were starting over in a new land.

South Philadelphia was a tough neighborhood, but it was also a place where the Cambodians could find a sense of community. They built temples and businesses, and they created a network of support for each other.

Adjusting to life in America was not easy for the Cambodians. They had to learn a new language, and they had to find jobs in a new economy. They also had to deal with the trauma of what they had experienced in Cambodia.

But the Cambodians were resilient. They worked hard, and they helped each other to succeed. They made South Philadelphia their home, and they helped to make the neighborhood a more vibrant and diverse place.

Sam, Srey, and their family did whatever it took to make a living. In the summer, they worked picking blueberries, driving tractors, and working in the packing house of a strawberry farm. They also picked peaches, worked in a greenhouse, a salad packing plant, and even did reporting for an insurance company. The children worked alongside their parents, and everyone contributed to the family's income.

Sam and Srey's journey to America was not easy. They had to leave their home country behind, and they had to start over in a new land. But they were determined to succeed, and they instilled their children with the same values.

Sam and Srey taught their children the importance of hard work, perseverance, and education. They also taught them the importance of family and community. These values helped the children to succeed in school and in their careers.

The children of Sam and Srey are now all successful professionals and business owners. They are all grateful for the values that their parents instilled in them, and they are proud to be Cambodian-Americans.

The family's story is a testament to the resilience of the human spirit. They faced many challenges, but they never gave up. They worked hard, and they were able to achieve their dreams.

SOPHEAK TOUCH

95

www.ingramcontent.com/pod-product-compliance
Lightning Source LLC
Chambersburg PA
CBHW071209120626
46546CB00006B/2481